Living a life filled with friendship, love, hard-work, loyalty, trustworthiness, and determination is what makes the world a better place. May all the children of the world find "Ubuntu". It is only then that we can all achieve true happiness in life.

Tererai Trent and Lori Grainger

4

It was another bright, sunny day on the savanna and Zandi was daydreaming under the shade of a majestic baobab tree. The savanna was bursting with activity, some could be seen, some only heard.

Zandi gazed upon the huge *baobab* tree and watched all the life unfolding within its umbrella-like branches. A family of monkeys groomed each other under the watchful eye of a shy chameleon. A trail of black ants marched determinedly up the enormous tree trunk. A beautiful green snake clung to a branch and waited for its dinner to pass by. Colorful birds gathered on the canopy and squawked loudly to one another. The *baobab* tree was a **friend** to all, opening its many arms to the creatures of the savanna.

Zandi thanked the *baobab* tree for befriending her too and allowing her to enjoy the cool ground beneath the spreading tree. She gathered up her *chamboko,* snapped it in the air to waken the lazy cattle, and headed home.

10

Zandi made the same journey home every day, but today the sweet scent of the savanna made her dawdle along the way. She spotted a herd of striped zebra grazing peacefully with their companions, the mighty wildebeest. Zandi watched as they mingled together and noticed how they **protected** each other from the ferocious animals of the savanna. Without each other, the zebra and wildebeest would be prey to lions, leopards, and cheetahs. The **friendship** they shared reminded Zandi of her own village and the need to hurry home.

Zandi walked through the Acacia woodlands along the bank of the Kanyati River. Suddenly, she was face-to-face with four pairs of eyes looking at her from one of the big branches of a *mukute* tree. The eyes belonged to four monkeys who darted away making a *kek-kek-kek* sound. Startled, Zandi turned and saw a big monkey licking clean her newly born *mwana*. Tiptoeing past the mother, Zandi noticed another family of monkeys gathering behind a giant anthill. The new mother joined the **loving** family who began to quibble over whose turn it was to cuddle the newborn. "*Kek-kek-kek*," Zandi said as she spread her arms sending a big hug to the monkeys.

Zandi continued and came across a long trail of big, red ants moving a gigantic object across the grassland. Carefully, Zandi knelt down and peered closely at the procession. The gigantic object was a dead grasshopper! "Wow!" exclaimed Zandi. Each ant used its tiny jaws to help carry the grasshopper to their colony. **Hard-working** soldier ants surrounded the precious meal, while others cleared the path. Through **teamwork,** these ants carried their heavy load efficiently and successfully. Zandi gently patted the ground and whispered, "Goodbye little ants. Safe travels."

Zandi realized she was late bringing the cattle home. Soon, Grandma Gogo would be calling her. She gazed into the colorful sky and saw an African fish eagle flying overhead holding a snake in its talons. Zandi wondered if the eagle was bringing food to its mate guarding the big nest on a cliff above the river. Before she could see the female eagle opening her mouth to receive the delicious dinner, she heard her dog Tiger barking. "Woof, woof," barked Tiger. "Where have you been? I've missed you!" Zandi smiled, realizing that just like the eagle, Tiger was a **loyal** and **trustworthy** companion. Sending a big kiss to the eagles, Zandi and Tiger ran on.

Soon, Zandi and Tiger came upon a moving rock. Looking closer, Zandi saw that the mysterious rock had legs and was dark and shiny. A **determined** little bug was gallantly pushing a pile of dung! "What a yummy feast for the **hard-working** dung beetle," cried Zandi. In awe she watched as the little beetle swiftly rolled the gigantic ball. Zandi winked at the dung beetle and hurried off towards her village.

Zandi wasn't far from the village when she heard her Grandma Gogo's high-pitched call. She was late and the cattle needed to be in the *kraal*. After safely securing the cattle, Zandi skipped to her Grandma Gogo's hut for a steaming dish of *okra* and *sadza*.

Under a bright moon, the whole family sat around an open fire and listened with amazement as Zandi shared her exciting day on the savanna. When Zandi finished describing her day, Grandma Gogo sighed, lifted up her old bones, and leaned on her *tsvimbo*. She looked at Zandi and in her creaky, whispery voice said, "You have discovered the true meaning of "*Ubuntu*." To achieve *Ubuntu*, you must be a friend to all, protect one another, care for all creatures, work together, contribute to your community, and be willing to try and never give up. Only then can you achieve true happiness in life."

24

Grandma Gogo blew Zandi a kiss, smiled, gathered her sleeping mat, and sauntered contently to her sleeping hut.